A gesticulator is born, not made.

To such, however, as have not been endowed by nature with a fine nervous organism, a few general rules may be useful.

It may be stated, generally, that all motion must proceed from the shoulder. Whilst a sentence is in suspension the hand may be raised to a height somewhat above the shoulder; and, at its completion, may be brought down to the level of the breast, and sometimes drawn somewhat across it, and even lie upon with the fingers in careless repose. In emphatic sentences the hand may come down upon any inanimate object in front – e.g., table, barrier, etc. – with a force given to it by the elbow and wrist combined.

To attain proficiency, carefully watch some good model of gesture, or practice before a mirror.

Action should never be exaggerated, and the gesticulations to be avoided are circular movements of the arms; diving into the pockets; pushing the tongue against the cheek; fixing the eyes on some point in the building; standing with the feet or knees pressed together; fidgeting with a bread pill or piece of twine between the fingers; and so forth.

Generally, assume an easy manner on making your appearance, and guard against all feelings of timidity. If your subject be a melancholy one, look grave and thoughtful; if cheerful, let your countenance be lit up with a smile; if merry, you may advance to a grin.

*Survey your audience confidingly but not
rudely; and be careful not to pick out any
particular person or persons in the audience for
your remarks, but speak to all equally.*

Resolution *requires an expression of deep thought, with thumb and first finger resting on lower lip; the head inclining towards the breast; eyes downcast; then a sudden lighting-up of the countenance; a striking of the breast over the heart or of the thigh and a sharp turn on both feet as if in eagerness to carry out the inner determination of the mind*

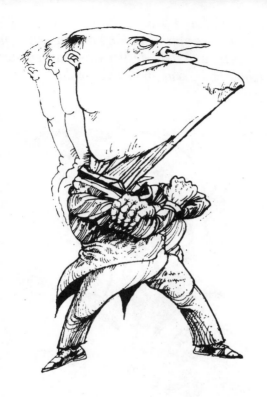

Obstinacy *requires an almost motionless attitude; a slight rocking may be allowed; eyes fixed, yet catching at anything said of an abnormal kind, and a visible attempt of the body to subdue the will.*

Fear *(which is a prospective affection)*
requires a voice almost lacking breath; open eyes;
wide mouth; and wild despairing countenance.
The whole body is apprehensive of danger.

Anger (*a sympathetic affection*) *demands a contracted brow; an impatient moving of the hands and arms inclining to violence or suppresed revenge; the breast heaves convulsively; and there is great muscular tension; the teeth grate; the foot stamps; and the fist is clenched.*

Pity *(a special sympathetic affection).* *Mixture of love and grief. Head inclined, with eyes looking up from under the lids; voice broken by sighs; a holding of the object's hand between both your own hands with slight up-and-down movement of the upper. In a gentleman there should be a visible effort to suppress tears; in a lady they should be encouraged.*

Jealousy (*mixture of passions opposed to each other*) requires a delineation of the several passions in turns. Hope, anger, fear, melancholy, despair, revenge, etc., have all to be brought in, and must be very rapidly, if not momentarily, delineated. It is only after excessive practice that this passion can be adequately represented.

Melancholy *(passive personal affection)*. Eyes cast down; every movement pensive; gloomy bearing altogether, with an utter disregard of all which goes on around. Sighs often break the utterance.

Joy *(active personal affection).* Voice rises and falls at random; smiling face with occasional exuburant clapping of hands; restlessness and rocking of whole frame, as if impatient to give freedom to pent-up feelings.

Love (*social sympathetic affection*). *Look of general satisfaction; every feature at its highest tension, with the gaze intently fixed on the beloved object; voice takes a winning, pathetic, rapturous turn. If unsuccessful, the tone becomes more persuasive, yet never coarse; and, if kneeling be necessary, one knee should only be employed, and that the farther one from the audience.*

Mirth *(active personal affection)* must be exuberant and implies tortuosity of the features, especially eyes, nose, and mouth; with convulsive laughter, and holding of sides.

And so we might go on to give gesture to every idea under the sun; but enough has been said to explain this part of the subject, which, as we have said before, can never be successful unless the aspirant have within him the necessary nervous force to make him an elocutionist. Unless he be possessed by nature of the "vis dramatica," all hopes of making an eminent actor, advocate, or divine should be abandoned.